Little Red

Little Red

Instagram: @creatively_elsie

ISBN: 978-1-7392109-0-8

Published by Ingram Spark

Little Red

**Poetry by
Ellie Craner**

Little Red

Author's note

Little Red is a collection of the poetry I wrote between the ages of fourteen and twenty three. Some of my older poems feel clumsy and embarrassing to share, but they are as much a part of my journey as my most recent writing. This collection explores my experiences with anxiety, mental health, love, relationships, mistakes I've made and the journey of getting to know myself. As a result, a number of these poems are very personal and have been a safe space for me to be my most vulnerable and creative self. This book is a time capsule, holding the person I used to be, the person I am, and also the person I am becoming. By the end of this book, I am hopeful that you will know me better than before you started.

This is the first book I am publishing of, I hope, many more. The first thing I can remember wanting to be as a child was an author who illustrates her own books. I am beyond excited that I've been able to make this dream a reality, and I am sincerely grateful to everyone that takes the time to read this book and go on this journey with me.

Little Red

Contents

Little Red

8

Into the woods
Part I

Into the woods

Little Red, take care
watch out and beware
as you enter into these woods.

For don't you see,
under cover of trees
and effervescent green
your shadows will lurk and thrive -

Distorted and strange
they may behave
in ways that fright and surprise.

These woods are a dangerous place
and through them you must make haste,
lest you be deceived, wronged
or thieved
by something with sharpened teeth.

So don your cloak, armour
and hope
that you make it out of these woods
alive.

When I say, want to read my poetry? I mean:
after @poetry.by.e

Here is a flash-light. Here is an insight into my mind. Highlight any decent parts you find. If you like. If you think it's any good. Is it any good? I mean: *here is the start of a ball of yarn, tug open the page and watch me fall apart. unravelled strings of (in)coherent syllables and sentences.* I mean: *here is a layer of skin I have shed. peel back each page waiting to be read.* I mean: *here is a history book. travel into the past with me and relive my memories. do you think I'm a reliable source?* When I say, want to read my poetry? I mean: *here is my heart on an operating table. here is a scalpel. be careful. criticism is sharp.* I mean: *I trust you.* I mean: *here is a magnifying glass. I want to be seen. loved. admired.* I mean: *do you think it's good enough?* I mean: *am I good enough?*

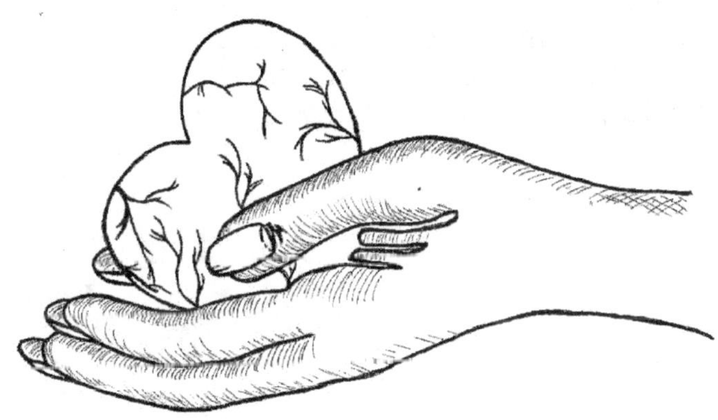

Reasons to write:

Because I can't say these words out loud.
Because I'm too shy.
Because the moment has passed -
But I'll share my words with you, if you ask.

- Vulnerability.

Because writing is like taking a photo.
A poem is a snapshot of how I felt in this moment
which will never come again,
is gone,
is here.
Saved.
I want to remember I felt this way.

- Preservation.

Because inside my mind is a ball of yarn
all jumbled and knotted,
a collection of all my thoughts and
to write is to take the end of the string
and gently tug
each thought
and lay it in a straight line,
untangling my mind.

- Decluttering.

Little Red

Because I want closure
and processing the past
might be the only way I find
some peace at last.

                                        - Rest.

Because sometimes nothing makes
any damn sense
unless I see the words on the page.
Introverted intuition isn't much good
at processing emotion.
It criticises and questions the validity of them -
why is it that I can respect a page
but not what goes on inside my brain?
I must release these feelings
and allow them to be,
free them from my harsh judgement
and distorted reality.

                                - Self protection.

Cells and Sea Foam

Did you know that salt water runs through my veins?
It doesn't trickle or drip;
I am no mere stream.
It courses like a roaring tide
flooding this body, this frame.
It tugs at me -
a current of cells and sea foam.

It's true, I have salt water in my veins.
Does this mean that when I cry, I bleed?

I cannot question
that part of me belongs to the water,
like a siren called to the deep.
But with hair like coral and eyes blue-green
in truth
I cannot tell you which part it is.

Hansel and Gretel

I'm leaving a trail of breadcrumbs,
letting the grains fall
through my fingers like sand.
Time takes me further away from you
but I hope this will lead me back.

When I lose my way
and I forget my roots,
I will follow this trail back home to you.

These scattered sentences I leave behind me,
these crumbs of poems and prose,
feel like a great unravelling.
Perhaps at the end of this journey I'll have
untangled my core.

Each step I take, I shed the weight
of an old heartache.
My footsteps become lighter,
my head, I hold higher
as I walk deeper into the woods.

Pungent Soul

I carry my spirit in a bottle.
These treasured traits and memories
are stored like a priceless perfume.
I loosen the stopper
and i n h a l e
but only for a moment -
lest any part of me should escape,
diffusing into the breeze
until it is no more.
Sweet notes of summer days
spent in retro cafes
mingle with the bitter scent of heartache
and forgotten dreams.
They press against the seams
of this bottle
struggling against their confinement.
Perhaps my soul is too pungent -
too full of vitality
to be encased in glass, apart from reality.
Perfectly preserved for appearance sake,
but all the while growing stale,
Perhaps life is too short to stifle creativity -
perhaps I should set
           my
             soul
               f r e e
and embrace all the sensations
this world has for me.

Little Red

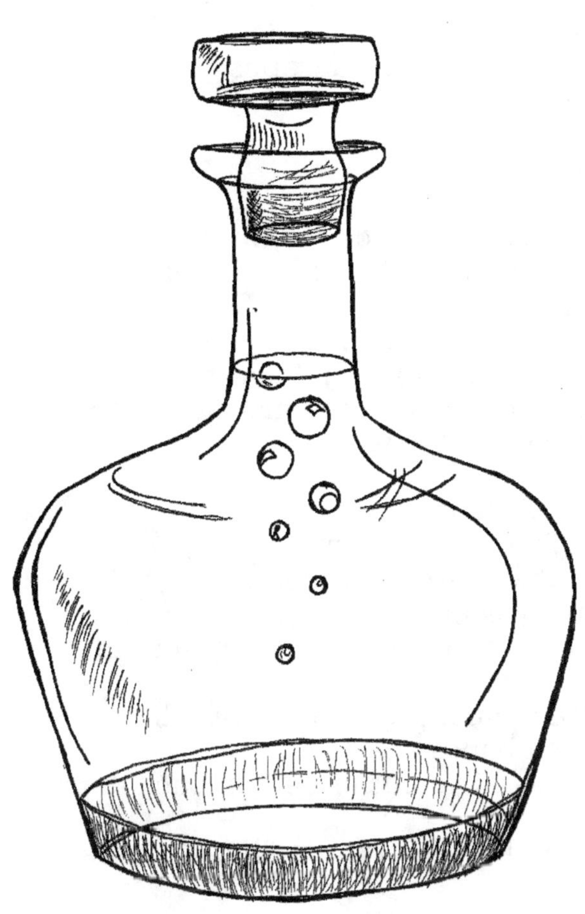

Weightless

I lose myself in books.
Leaving my body slumped on the couch
my soul slips between the sheets of paper.
I become entangled in paragraphs,
immersed in ink
until I no longer exist-
One with the narrative.

I hover weightlessly beside the hero
as I follow their trials, their heartbreaks
so real it hurts.
I cheer for them, I mourn with them
to the point I think they might sense me
in the pauses between their constructed dialogue
hanging on their every word.

And then the book finishes
and I'm left facing a dead end.
The hero waltzes through the back page
to their happily ever after
and I have no choice but to come up for air.

It takes me a moment to redress myself
in my skin and bones.
Sometimes I feel I've put myself on back to front
or inside out
and I'm left with a lingering feeling of nausea.

Little Red

I'm disconnected.
Disassociated.
Stuffed inside a body so limited
it can only exist in one time, one place.
I steady my breath
and reach for the next book.
Longing to be weightless again.

She's been captured

She's been captured, you say with a sigh
and a roll of the eyes.
Who knows when she'll be free?

At least she's comfortable, I shrug.
Curled up on an old leather couch,
she could do worse.

She says nothing.

Her hands are bound to the book in her lap
and though her face is quite still,
her eyes are a mirror of expression.

You say you don't understand
how printed letters can have so much power
as to render man speechless.

It would be a mistake to take her stillness
for weakness, I reply.
She's armed with the knowledge of a hundred worlds
and she's lived a thousand lives.

Sometimes it takes surrendering
for a moment
to be truly free.

She writes

She writes.
Pen in hand,
hand on paper.

Lacing ink across the page
she loops her letters;
perfecting her craft.

Once completed she lifts it triumphantly to the light,
before cradling her masterpiece as it takes
it's first breath.

Creativity incarnate

Birth is messy.
The infant cries and garbles
of prose
unintelligible-
and yet as these poems wave
their chubby fingers in the air,
firmly grasping your own,
in this moment creativity is
tangible.
They have a lifetime to be refined,
but for now,
let's just revel in their innocence.

She wants to be beautiful

She wants to be beautiful,
but not like in the magazines.
Although beautiful the models may be
they are things of fiction and photo-shop.

She wants to be beautiful,
to thrive in her own skin.
Rather than to squeeze and prod and frown
at the excess baggage she's told she carries.

She wants to be beautiful,
to be called more than just pretty.
Pretty is a compliment. Pretty is sweet.
Pretty is indifferent. Average.

She wants to be beautiful.
Beautiful is unique.
Beautiful is passionate.
Beautiful is to be adored.

She wants to be beautiful
In a world where perfection is always out of reach.

Old Soul

I belong to a Jane Austen novel.
The romance of the past lingers on my skin
like old perfume,
still fragrant and sweet.

I long for love letters, written in prose,
with such extravagance and intention
that they require no Persuasion
to write to me.

Instead I get texts - on occasion
when they can be bothered,
written in shorthand
so I take up as little time
as possible.
Kept at arms length
so as not to wound their Pride
or Prejudice.

I am worth so much more.

I have an old soul, though young in spirit.
I am too full of vitality to be confined to the
Sense and Sensibility of the present.

Her Paper Heart

She has a paper heart
fluttering in her chest.
It's not crisp or white,
it's no hollow origami shell.

Her heart is stained
with the murmurings of her mind,
written in a deep dark ink.
It seeps through her veins, escaping
through her eyes
and bleeding into the tattoos on her skin.

She has a paper heart
beating in her chest.
Not weak or torn as many would like.
It gives life to her paper lungs
inflating them like lanterns
so she may breathe the words
so engraved into her soul
and set them free on the wind.

These little moments

The first waking moments after a good dream,
the crunch underfoot of a crispy leaf.
Looking in the mirror, seeing past the acne scars,
listening to slow electric guitars.
Feeling comfortable, liking the way I'm looking,
dancing in the kitchen while dinner is cooking.
Curled up on my bed at the end of the day,
turning my pillow to the cool side, 'hitting the hay'.
A bubble bath when the temperature is just right,
watching Pride and Prejudice for the hundredth time.
Discovering new music, harmonies and lyrics,
painting on a canvas with my acrylics.
Banana pancakes on a Saturday morning,
the spark of magic when a poem is forming.
Creativity moving softly, day and night,
words breathing their first life in the first light.
Weary eyes watching the sun start to rise,
returning colour to the world.
Stretching, uncurled, I can't help but smile.
These little moments make the everyday worthwhile.

I captured the moon

I captured the moon last night.
Amongst the shadows and indigo hues
I tethered a lasso
and aimed for the stars.

At last it was within my grasp,
this holographic muse of poetry and art.
Tell me, what secrets does your dark side hold?
Your story need not be left untold.

Won't you wait - stay for a while?
Me on the ground, you in the sky.
When dawn arrives, don't cover up your eyes
for I will adorn you with stardust.

Neon Nights

I find no relief in starlit dreams
when reality is bursting at the seams,
unable to relinquish its grip on me.
Down city streets,
my sleepless soul wanders alone
as I search for you, my home,
under every street light.
These neon signs are electric lifelines;
islands in the dark.
But I feel a deep burn blue
every night I don't find you
among the castaways.
Are you a dreamer?
Spiral spinning between the stars
flying so fast gravity has no hold on you?
Would you let me be your anchor,
a flesh and blood tether to this world?
Would you help me breathe
and shed the weight that
causes this realist's heart to ache?
Would you help me leave the ground,
heaven bound,
until I'm caught up in your orbit?

Little Monsters

All we want
is for the world to love the little monsters we are.
Stomping feet and chomping teeth,
we run rampant in the moonlight.
By day we hide, we wear our human disguise,
only slipping briefly as we greedily
scoop our fingers around the edge of the mixing bowl
to get at the final traces of cookie dough.

We have childish thoughts
and childish smirks
that sulk when our inner adult scolds us.

We're messy, muddy, moody little monsters.
We're quirky and creative.
We like to play 'let's pretend',
dressing up in skirts and suits.
We wear painted smiles and polished shoes,
as if we have a clue how to navigate this
grown up facade,
when in fact we're just waiting
to meet someone
who gets our kind of crazy.

Heartbeat

Write me in the space between your ribs.
Write my name on the hidden places
which beat
for me
only.

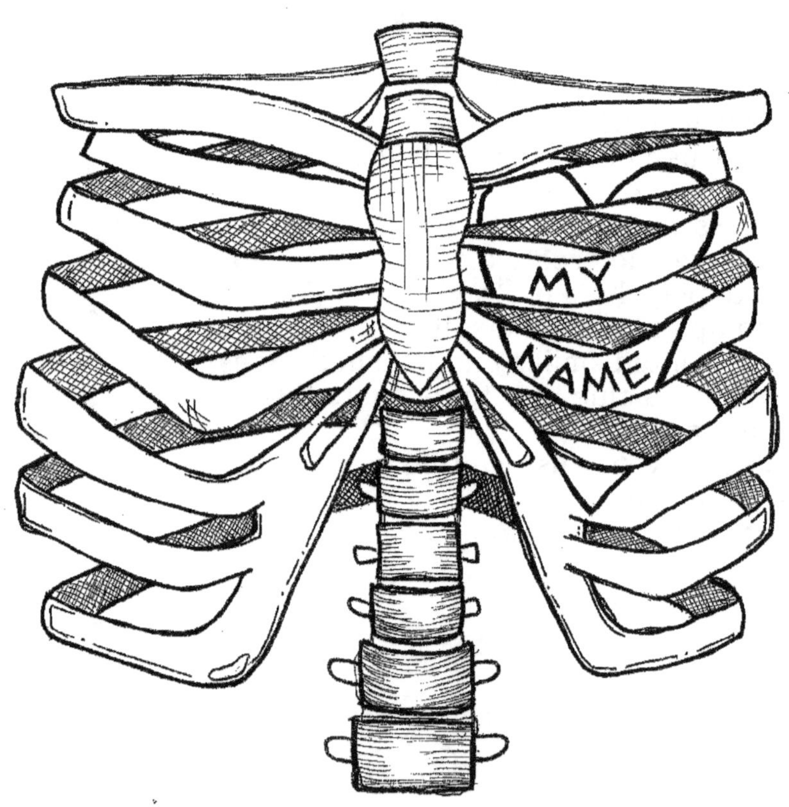

Excavation

A poet's quest:
To excavate buried secrets of the heart
with the scratching of quills
and gentle bleeding of ink.

Chemical Hearts

The place between wake and sleep.
The moment after the jump
but before   the
fall
A breath, held in suspense -
Limbo.

Somewhere between heartache
and healing our adolescent wounds
we are expected to find ourselves;
A chemical   compass
mapping the desires
of our teenage hearts.

Somewhere between overalls and offices
is a place like the space under our beds,
collecting dust in the shadows   of our hearts;
we hide our mess with the monsters
we're still afraid of.

If we are to escape eternal lingering
in the great 'might have been'
of   our hopes and
                                                  dreams,
we must make peace with the hormones
running rampant through our veins.
We must see through the lies
our distorted eyes feed us
as we walk this hall of mirrors
to   our ever afters.

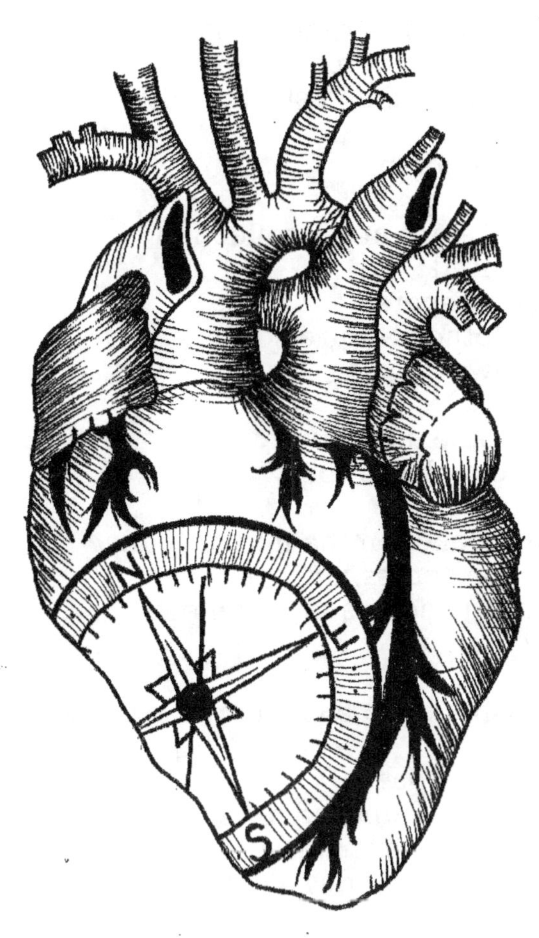

Acne

My skin is a battlefield.
Littered with scars of struggles past.
The rubble is barely swept away
before my pores swell and stretch with the onset
of a new month.
A chemical time bomb.

I can't help but stare at my reflection
and poke and prod
(with sterilised fingers)
at the faults Mother Nature so
gleefully bestows.

If all bodies are beautiful,
why does mine feel less so?

I cried when I looked in the mirror today
at the landscape across my face.
A mountain range across my forehead,
a constellation on my chin.

My cheeks flush a deep burning red as instead
I look away
unable to meet my gaze.
Its been over three hundred days
and still these marks remain,
new ones forming everyday.

I don't feel beautiful.
I don't feel comfortable.
And I am exhausted.

Little Red

I'm doing all the right things
and yet they seem to bring no change.

So don't look at me.
Or if you must, meet only my gaze
and don't let your eyes wander
around my face.

Please.

Goosebumps

You reach for me in the dark,
feeling for my silhouette
as if to check I'm still there
and not merely a shadow;
a murky impression of last night.

Your arms wrap around me,
drawing me closer until we breathe as one.
A sensation so intimate it gives me goosebumps
which you trace like Braille.

So study me well
and take it all in,
I am not so easy to read
in the daylight.

Little Red

Little Red

The Wolves
Part II

The Wolves

Little Red, take care
watch out and beware
as you journey through these woods.

Don't venture off the beaten path
listen carefully and don't stray too far,
for though you see intrigue and beauty
hidden behind lie grins most sharp and toothy -

Little Red, distorted and strange,
you may behave
in ways that might surprise you.

These wolves are dangerous people.
All charm and beguile, they'll lead you on,
all the while you grow ever lost.
Not that you'll care.
Not that you'll mind.
As long as they don't leave you behind -

Little Red, take care
keep your gaze on the path ahead and stare.
Don't look at, don't listen to, and don't engage
with any wolves that come your way
lest you be distracted, or even remotely attracted
to the pairs of dark eyes that follow you -

Little Red ... where are you going?
I know you're innocently hoping
for a different ending to the one so plain.
I could tell you again – but what's the use?
You think you know better than truth.

Little Red

Little Red, if you're truly set on going ahead
with this misguided detour
I only pray you've secured your cloak, armour
and hope
that you make it out of these woods
alive.

2014

They started on the bus.
A rickety thing, in pretty bad shape,
the headlights were secured with pieces of tape.
It had peeling paint and sticky seats,
but back then it was a real treat
if I got to give my legs a rest,
rucksack hugged to my chest,
as I travelled to school.

Most days I barely made it through the doors,
legal limits blatantly ignored;
regularly 15 standing and 20 more.
We were packed liked sardines into these
tiny tin can machines.

There were always
people pressed
to my sides,
back and front,
no where to hide-
and always too loud.
Too much shouting, screaming
The aisles were teaming
with children running wild.

A jungle of limbs and animals cries,
teenage boys would laugh in surprise
when I'd push them away
with a weary face
after they'd stumbled into me
for the tenth time.

Little Red

Elbowing my ribs.
Stomping on my feet.
I couldn't stand the sweat and the heat.

I was easy prey for pranks and jokes -
if you think its funny to lift a girls skirt
Or try and set her seat. her hair. on fire
or even dare to call her a liar
when she's in tears because a boy has hit her
in the face with a condom water balloon
when all she wanted was to be left alone
on the journey home,
but now everyone's laughing
and she can't get away.

When I look back, I'm not surprised
that this was enough to eventually trigger
my first panic attack.
They started on the bus.

When I say, I'm having a panic attack, I mean:

i'm experiencing a biopsychological reaction to an internal or external stressor. my sympathetic nervous system has triggered my fight or flight response and i need to get out of here. I mean: my adrenaline and cortisol levels are increasing - are coursing through my body and i can't stop my hands from shaking. stop. *please stop shaking*. I mean: there is a balloon expanding in my chest and it's pressing on my lungs. do you have a pin? I mean: i've become aware of my heartbeat. it's moving from my chest, clawing its way up my throat. I mean: i'm stuck inside my mind and i can't find the exit. the button marked 'escape' does nothing when i press it. *can you hear me yelling?* i can't seem to make a sound and yet there's too much noise. i'm drowning in it. *i'm drowning* - I mean: i'm a detective. tracing the clues that led to this moment. was it one thing or many? if i exclude the impossible, will the reasons left, however improbable, give me any peace of mind? I mean: i'm a judge. Are my feelings valid? do I allow myself to have it, this moment? I mean: i'm about to cry. you can leave if it makes you uncomfortable. i've had enough of these to know i'll be okay. I mean: i'm not okay. i want you to stay. I mean: my parasympathetic system will be kicking in any time now. it'll calm down my heart, stop this mess, this falling apart. I mean: the adrenaline is slowing, my lungs are expanding, pupils enlarging, i'm even smiling. look my hands have stopped shaking. not really. I mean: help me. p*lease*. all I really need is a hug. that would be enough. i can handle the rest.

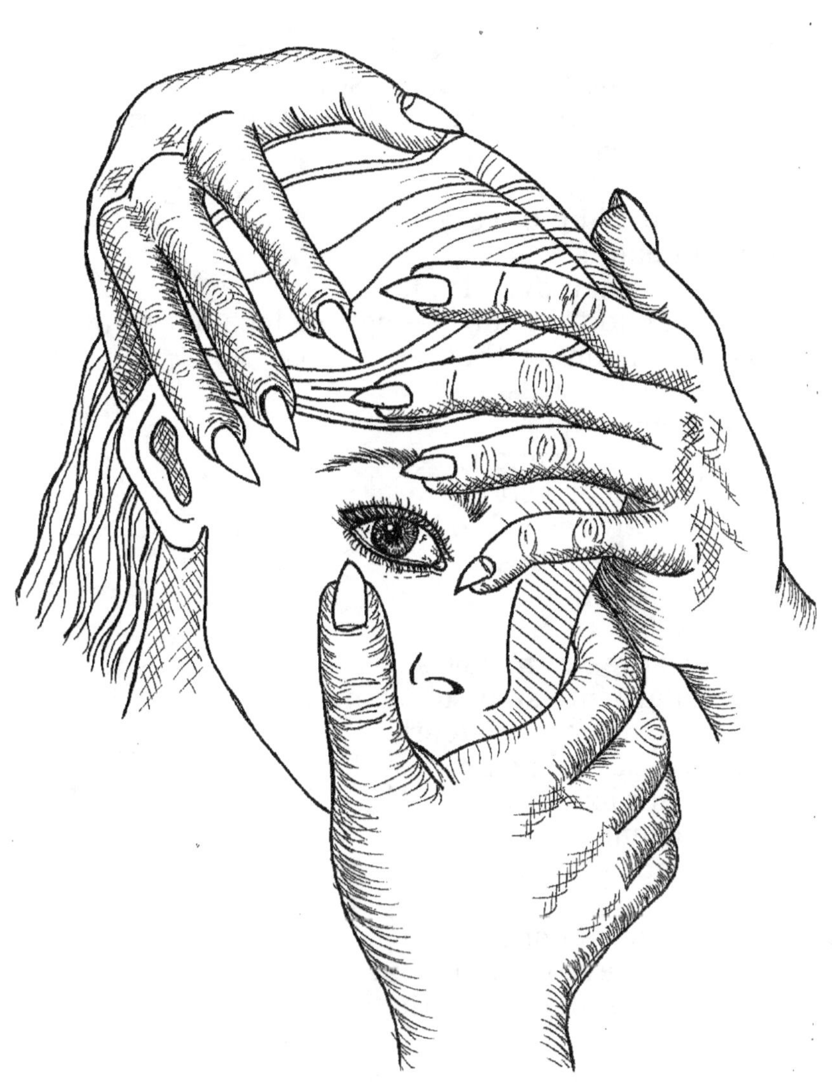

Her

Standing at the mirror I see her, the girl
Always standing too close, too still.
Breathing down my neck, her presence lingers -
She will not leave.

My breath fogs up the glass.
It is not enough;
I cannot hide her, disguise her
I can't- I cannot put her in a box, or lock her away.
She is too human for that.

Donning my makeup;
I perform the morning ritual
Mascara, blusher, *more.*
Lest I remotely resemble her ashen face,
Her tightly drawn lips.
No, I am not her.

Those eyes are not my eyes,
I cannot glare into souls like her.
Those teeth are not my teeth,
Though the girl mimics me well.
She bites her lower lip -
Oh so innocent.
I am not her.

I once considered offering a truce,
But it would have been in vain.
It's true; she understands the fear, my panic.
She knows.
But she also watches as I drown.

Fading; softly, quickly
Is that her reflection I see, or mine?
I bite my lower lip. Could I be her?

Mascara, blusher, *more.*
No, I am—not her

No –

Rapunzel, Rapunzel

I remember the days spent in my tower,
life passing me by with every setting of the sun.
I used to sit on the window ledge
waiting for the day I might test my wings.

I remember the day you arrived,
dressed in your armour and brandishing a smile;
a fitting disguise.
It had seemed an ordinary day,

and it was the last of its kind.

You scaled my tower, inviting yourself in –
not that I minded; your company was pleasant.
I'd sit and listen late into the night
to the tales you'd tell of your valiant fights.

I remember the day, you coaxed me to the edge of my
tower,
the edge of my realm, my nest.
With your fingers you traced the horizon,
the silhouettes of a far off land,
before looking back at me, and down at me,
holding out your hand.

A perfected look of concern and pity was all I needed
for you to persuade me that I somehow needed rescuing
from the tower I, myself, had built.

Bright lights

Fireflies and your eyes
illuminated under starlight
and suddenly I forget how to breathe -

You are

We all crave magic and a
little madness –
you are enough for me.

My Safe Place

You were like roses.
Your petals red like the flags I ignored -
Silky smooth.
They concealed the thorns in your side
now in mine too.
My safe place.

Over time you dropped your petals
your niceties, your charms.
One by one you let them fall
revealing your true form.
Oh how I mourned my safe place.
But now your thorns were rooted
in me
and I found I could not leave.

I tried to stick your petals back on
but I only made my fingers bleed -
Red like roses
My safe place.
I don't know how to leave.

53

A conversation of limbs

We lie side by side
under the lamplight
trying to decipher each other.
We untangle limbs and mixed messages,
but we don't seem to speak the same
love languages.

You talk with your touch,
your hands running down my spine
until every bone caves to your touch;
melting, aching until it's all too much
and shivers ripple across my skin.

I hear you.
I do.
I hear you.

I try in vain, again and again
to lavish you with compliments and prose.
My words would rival tales of old,
but still they fall on deaf ears.
Your mind is elsewhere, it's pre-occupied.
My mouth runs dry at the sight of your
vacant eyes.

How can I get you to believe
that the best way to love me
is to simply be
by my side?

Little Red

The only gift I want is your time.
To know that you enjoy my company
and are not easily bored of me -
or my love.

I run my fingers through your hair
and all at once I'm caught in your stare
as I bring you back to the room
with such intensity
I know it will be the end of me.

So I surrender again
to a conversation of limbs;
it seems the only way I can win
is to love your way first
and hope you'll hear me
on the other side.

Rain's rhythm

There's something about the pouring rain,
that makes me want to burn.
Dancing barefoot in the grass
to the rhythm of thunder claps.

The heavier the rain
the more smoke billows from me.
I dance as the flames are extinguished
and my burns are soothed -
until the next time I play with fire.

In the fire

Have you noticed how time slows down
in the moments before an accident?
A collision?
The seconds are stretched thin
before the inevitable occurs.
The edges of reality fraying at the seams
as fate hangs by a thread,
and then it happens.
and then it's over.
and all that's left is the aftermath.
Like two cars that have crashed -
shades of orange and crimson
reflect on shards of broken glass,
a fiery mosaic.
But what if instead of a collision
there was just you and I,
locking eyes across a crowded room
as everything grinds to a standstill.

All that we said

"I don't know how you managed to be a combination of all
my favourite things."
"You're so wonderful."

Pretty words.
Kind words.
Lovely words.

"Mine?"
"Yours."

Pretty words.
Short words.
Silence.

Tired eyes
ragged breaths
hearts beating faster.

Adrenaline coursing
tears pouring
time slows down.

"You ok?"
"Yeah. You?"

Short words.
Sharp words.

Silence.

Internal Groan

I have
no words.
Nothing to say.
Nothing that would make you understand
for you refuse to feel.
So how could words ever reach you?
Words; curved lines, jagged lines, lifeless lines.
Words would never reach you.
And yet I find myself writing, writing, writing.
Tring to give a voice to the ache in my stomach
that churns and constricts -
A voice to the headache that steals my thoughts,
my dreams.
A voice to the tears,
though silently shed, they *scream*.
I can't help but write.
But you -
you talk.
What are you voicing?
For you refuse to feel.
Talking with your mouth
so disconnected from your internal groan.
Do you lie with your eyes too?
Feel, damn it.
Cry with me, ache with me
mourn for our future lost.
If you are to talk
give life to your words.
Make me understand
or else your words will never reach me.

Wishes

Wishes are costly
and should not be made lightly.
We snuff the life from dandelions
in a single
breath
and watch the ashes scatter
as we imprint wishes
upon their bones.

Comets fall into our atmosphere
plummeting under the weight of
whispered words and expectations
until their magic is released
in a holographic blaze-
and then they are no more.

I would have uprooted the earth
and torn apart the stars
if it had meant
I could keep you,
but oh what a terrible price
we would have paid.

Persistent as the tide

The process of erosion takes time.
A cliff is not demolished by a single wave,
it takes grit and stones
repeatedly hurled at it's base
to break down its foundations.

You have eroded me,
softly, slowly.
You dragged your calloused fingertips
repeatedly over my covered skin
until my no became nothing
and you took my silence for consent.
Did I want this?
You gave me no time to think.

You wore down my defences
with kisses and whispers of
"how bad could it be?"
till my morals were on their knees
before you.

And I fell-
all at once and so completely
crumbling into the sea
drowning out all reason.
It was only when I later resurfaced,
in the dark of my empty room
that I let my tears fall.

No matter how I tried to rebuild,
my waterlogged body was never strong enough
to refuse -

Little Red

and when you'd had your fun
my destruction continued still.
Pummelled by the thoughts and words
of a younger, disappointed me.

I realise now that it was never a matter of
whether I did or did not want to.
I'm not a saint, only human at best,
but I said I wouldn't go there from the start.

You claimed to respect that -
all the while wearing me down
like the way you ran your thumb over
my knuckles with a smile.
Softly, slowly,
persistent as the tide.

Leftovers

What do you do with leftover love.
These feelings with nowhere to go?

They seem fated to grow cold and stale
inside my chest,
but perhaps it's for the best
that they remain locked up,

lest we look back on all we lost
and crumble under the weight of our
silence.

This leftover love will sustain me
until I have had my fill of your memory
and I am content to waste away.

Gardening

I must stop digging up the past
expecting to find fresh roses.

I must stop watering these memories
with tears,
trying to bring life to seeds
that have long decayed.

The cost of saving myself

Poetry is raw.
Formed from the groans our hearts utter-
It will not be silenced.

Poetry lurks in the darkest corners of our minds
conjuring metaphors and similes
the most vibrant of imagery
as our pain desperately tries to be understood.
It will not be silenced.

You are my poetry
My muse.
The embodiment of all the hurt I feel.

I could not understand you.
Your labyrinth of juxtapositions
still have me turning in circles.
And now that you're gone,
I still cannot leave.

The pain your memory inflicts
beats verses out of me
until I am black and blue
and yet I still write.

If I were to move on,
let you lie half in your grave
to save myself,
would it cost me my creativity?

Little mermaid

I surrendered my voice
to be by your side,
fighting against the tide
and pull of the truth,
that I was not meant for you.
Dipping your toes in the water
you claimed to have experienced the ocean.
You said you didn't need it.
I said I didn't mind, that it was fine -
all the while walking the thin line
between the waves and the shore
unsure of which side I belonged -
I suppressed the best parts of me
to try and get you to see
my worth on your terms.
My sea foam footprints dissolved eventually
along with my resolve to keep sacrificing
my voice for your comfort.
If you were to see me,
as I truly am
I fear you would drown.
Some creatures are not meant to
experience such depths.

I, The Original

You told me that you were scared
you would never find someone else.
Someone like me.
I said that you wouldn't.
Not to be sassy, not so I could 'win' the breakup,
but because it's a fact.

There is no one else like me.
No one else with the unique combination
of features and traits that I possess.

You meant it as a compliment, I suppose,
that I was such a thing you'd want to find again.
It was more painful that I, the original,
was not worth your efforts.

You lost me,
so don't try to soften the blow by finding a replacement.
Anyone else will be a dull comparison of what I was.

Of what I am.

Last request

Break my heart quickly
and leave me lonely.
There's nothing worse than
suffocating slowly.

I'd rather the ocean pull me under
so I can fight for my breath
than not realise the waters have risen to my neck.
The numbness set in so gradually
that I don't realise I can't swim
until its too late.

So take the ground from under my feet
and don't break my fall.
Don't be the one to support me
through it all
or else I'll never be able to sort
through these broken pieces
and separate the parts of you from me.

Let me cry so I can feel.
Let me bleed so I can heal.
Walk away and don't leave me attached.
Walk away and don't look back.

I'll be alright.

No.

"No." I whispered.
It's a small word,
a short word,
but its power made me tremble.

No.
I would not let you use me again,
picking me up like a remote whose buttons you could press
for a hug or a kiss,
rewinding us to the past -
only to lose me later between the sofa cushions
or perhaps under the coffee table.
Careless.
No.
I would not submit to your double standards any longer.

"No." I said a little louder.

Your eyes widened.
Not the apology you were expecting.
The only apology I'll make
is for taking so long to stand up for myself.
I walk out of your room and for the first time
I don't look back.

No.
It's a short word
but its power made me tremble.

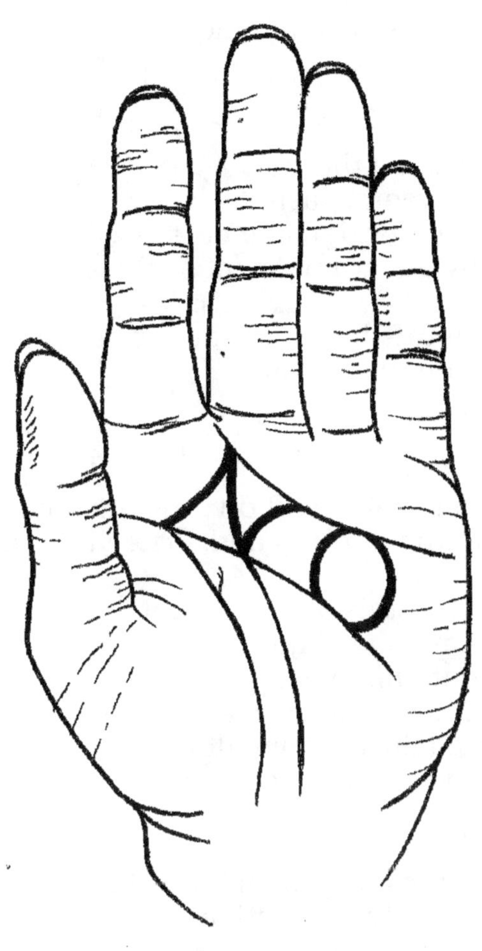

Passengers

We are passengers on separate trains
running parallel in opposite lanes.

Mind the gap.

It doesn't seem to be that far,
but distance between hearts
creates chasms no bridge can cross -
but occasionally our trains meet at the same stop.

Our differing morals have me caught between tracks
stranded between platforms -

Mind the gap.

At some point our paths will diverge and change
until then I fog up the glass and write your name.

Travelling through this sun set night
our flickering carriages light
up and I see your silhouette.
Oh how well I know your frame.
I press my ear against the window
trying to hear every word you say.

We are parallels;
distorted reflections portraying a bad connection.
I know we have different destinations.
But if someday you'd like to meet,
cross the platform and finally greet -

Mind the gap.

Little Red

Long distance

Hey.
It's me.

I'm sorry. I know I said I'd call -
but life got in the way and I was
busy trying to survive it all.
You know how it is.
You always understand.

I know I could have – should have
come to you with these things.
You've promised to take them from me,
you always carry these aches more easily,
but without them I'll be empty handed.
This pain has become such a part of me
I don't know who or what I'll be without it,
and I can't stand the thought of the unknown.

Which is crazy,
because I left everything,
gave up the thing I wanted most – for you.
So why is my back still turned to the truth?
Perhaps I've ignored you for too long.
Perhaps I've squashed you so far down inside
and suppressed this identity of mine
that I don't know how to get back.

And – and I think I need help.

Little Red

Tell me, if I seek, then will I find?
Won't you open up these eyes so blind
to the truth that eludes me
on sleepless nights like these?

Tell me what's wrong with me. *Please.*

If I knock, I know you await
only to tell me it's too late
to take the painless road back to
you.

Won't you tell me why I built this wall between us?
What hurt am I hiding, buried so deep it escapes
internal reflection,
only surfacing to grip my heart and *squeeze.*

If your word is alive, why am I deprived of your presence?
What must I do to restart this heart of mine,
take it back in time to a place where I could say
"it is well with my soul" -

I know I said I'd call.

You'd think I'd even be able to leave a message
But here I am writing this letter
because I am too damn choked up to speak
to you,
God.

The crowded room

Me, myself and I.
My heart, body and mind.
We all occupy the same space
trying desperately to find our place,
twisting and contorting.
I am off balance -
Tilting.
      Stumbling.
         Falling.

I remember a time we were strangers,
now we're starting to look like familiar faces.
Old friends, reconnecting again.
How have you been?

I remember the night I lay in bed
squirming, trying to climb out of my own head,
out of my body
not my body.
not my body.
let me out.

Waves of nausea rolled over me
as the weight of reality
pulled me under.
My body, mind and heart
had wandered so far apart
I no longer recognised myself.
My body in my bed,
my heart in the room upstairs,
and my mind seething in disgust
at us both.

Little Red

A stranger in my own frame,
I had compromised myself again
and again
and what was left was unrecognisable
was numb.
And it needed to be,
or else I might not have survived the internal beating.

It takes a lot of energy to be disappointed in yourself,
to hate, even.

So uncomfortable in my own skin
until the day I was able to begin
to reclaim myself.
A redecorating, from the outside in.
This is me.
This is mine.
My body.
My heart.
My mind.

I will make room for us all.

Baby blue

Blue is scarred with grey
and I can't stop the sky from
crying.

Emergence
Part III

Emergence

Little Red, take care
watch out and beware
as you emerge from these darkened woods.

When you finally flee from
under the cover of trees
and shadows that seem to breathe
don't you dare look back.
You've circled around, stood your ground
but this was never a battle you could win.
These woods are not your home.

Oh distorted and strange,
they certainly behaved
in ways that so surprised -
I know that your eyes deceived you.

Exterior dangers, interior deception.
What can you trust when you own perception is flawed?
Blurry boundaries and wrong compromise
filled the gaps self love should have occupied,
but now you're doing what you know is right,
things will seem a little brighter.

So run, Little Red, run,
back towards the path, back towards the sun,
and don't let anything distract you.
For this world is filled with woods and wolves
and things that will pull you in all directions.
But if you've learnt your lesson and made progression
in prioritising your morals and heart,
you'll smile and wave and be on your way
sticking to the narrow path.

Little Red

You've donned your armour and cloak,
but I hope that you won't be afraid to loosen the knots
so tightly bound around your throat.

Little Red, I hope, that someday you'll
let down your guard and uncover your scars
for someone who'll love you as you are.
For someone who'll also reveal their heart
in full, not in part, not hiding behind a mask.

I paint my past with poetry

I paint my past with poetry.
With soft sibilance I wash away harsh yesterdays
and soothe my tear soaked heart.

With caesura I
fracture
my words my
train of thought.
I pack the past into
bite
sized chunks
so I do not over indulge
the what ifs.

With the imagery of similes
I store my memories within relatable scenes,
not quite as they seem,
so I may keep them at arms length,
like a box of old toys
you don't have the strength to part with.

I scrub and I clean, and yet it still seems
I am not rid of my shadows.
I am tainted by memories of you,
my muse.

Tell me,
how many poems will it take
to sever the roots you have
dug
into my creativity?

For now

Stop!
Stop there.
       That's close enough -
       for now.

Ok.
Maybe one step closer
         and a half
           but that's it -
           for now.

Here's a window.
I'll open a curtain for you, let you peer through into
my life.
What do you think? (it's a bit of a mess, right?)
The last person I let in didn't bother to tidy before they
left.
I'm trying my best though.

I'll meet you by the window,
              maybe open it a little.
There's no door yet.
I'm afraid I can't let you in -
for now.
But perhaps if I make a door
we could talk through it.

Me on one side
        You on the other?

I should offer you a drink,
I think that's what good hosts do, right?

Little Red

I wonder what you will offer me.
Perhaps (if you're patient) I'll make you a key.

A key for a door
which will let you in, let you know more.
If you want to. (no pressure though.)

Stop.
        Please.
                That's close enough.

I promise you I'm not hard to love,
I just need to be shown that I can trust you.
There's so much more than what you can see
I'm trying (so hard) to be the best I can be,
but you have to earn it.
I'm worth it.
But I can't just let anybody in.
Not again.

Stop.
        That's close enough.
                        For now.

To bury the dead

This morning I saw a ghost in the mirror.
Fogged with icy breath,
I rubbed my sleeve, trying to see her clearer.

She carried a suitcase, battered and worn.
I knew all too well the contents
though I could have sworn
I threw it away a long time ago.

Oh. Its you.
Weren't you buried?
Aren't we through
with this haunting?

She took a seat on the edge of my bed,
telling me it's not so easy to shed
the weight of memory and ache.
It takes more than a funeral to bury the dead.

I sat down with a sigh,
keeping an eye on the suitcase.
This was simply not the time or place
to unpack all this again.

How many times must we do this dance?
I've learnt all I can from my past.
I've cried and mourned,
I've weathered the storms.
I've actually been fine for quite some time -
What else can you possibly have to say?

It's okay, she smiled.
It's okay that it hurts again today.

Little Red

There's no deadline for healing,
there's no shame in feeling what you do.
Something you're carrying is bothering you,
let's take a look together and work it through.
This might be easy to solve, but in case it's not
be kind to yourself today.

We opened the case and started to explore
my memories of the hurt, battered and worn.
I'll be kind to myself today.
By the time I surfaced for air
she'd already faded away.

She dances

She dances softly,
swaying from side to side
to a silent melody
that has the rhythm of a heartbeat

She dances alone,
one half of a waltz
turning in circles
like a figure on a music box

She dances in the shadows,
weaving between former silhouettes,
now but tricks of the moonlight
that fade with the dawn.

Caged

Oh little bluebird, why so blue, bird?
Have you lost your song?
Did it slip between the cage
it's wistful melody floating far away from you?

Oh little bluebird, is it true, bird,
that you saw the view freedom had to offer
and flew right back under cover of your cage?

Oh little bluebird, won't you sing a tune, bird
under these bright lights?
Always on display, these vertical lines are getting in your
way -
Is it your love of comfort that holds you back?

Oh little bluebird, don't you know it's true, bird,
that you don't have to wait
for the one who says they have the key?
Lift the latch little bluebird,

It's time to set yourself free.

Love's memory

I have imagined what love looks like so often
it feels like a memory.
I have imagined love on the faces
of people in far away places
who will never know my name.

I have created fictional narratives to rival
the greatest of love stories
all within the safety of my mind
with the assurance of a happily ever after.

I have read about what love looks like and
I'm often surprised
I've yet to stumble into an inciting incident.
One where I'll meet my counterpart by coincidence,
and we'll be inseparable thereafter.

My character is still being set up,
my backstory is just being filled in,
I know this is necessary before my story can begin.

I thought I knew love at 18
so I gave my heart to a boy
dressed like a man.
It was unplanned,
as was the breech of my boundaries.
Taken apart one by one until I was dismantled.
Why sneak in the window, when you can remove the walls?
He took it all and left
having completed the theft.

I have imagined what love looks like so often -
but now I am uncertain.

Little Red

Love lacks a face, a name
and every time I fill it in I am reminded of the pain
that came with being vulnerable.

I'm walking with crutches made of daydreams.
I'm clinging to emotional walls
and yet I wonder if I'm setting myself up to fall.
Again.
It's a long way down.

Will love reach out a hand to help me stand
and will I recognise it if it does?
Will it feel like an old friend?
Or will my perceptions have to end in order
to let the truth in?
Can I lean on love?
Will it help me up?
I have imagined what love looks like so often
it feels like a memory.
I wonder if love will remember me too.

Those Three Little Words

Those three little words
are like water to a parched soul.
A lyrical oasis in this desert world,
restoring life to these brittle bones.

To hear and speak these three little words
is to breathe -
a cyclical movement
through my lungs, my frame.

Without them I am suffocating.
The absence brings silence,
stale air in my chest
building heavy pressure.
I wonder if you feel the same.

A well that has dried up;
my lips are chapped
unable to speak those three little words
to anyone.

My mouth is unable to form the shapes
of this foreign language.
My teeth grind and pierce my tongue
and all the while my heart speaks in groans.

If I am ever to break free,
the one I must first confess to
must be me.
For without self love I cannot heal,
cannot move forwards
and I will wander through this desert alone.

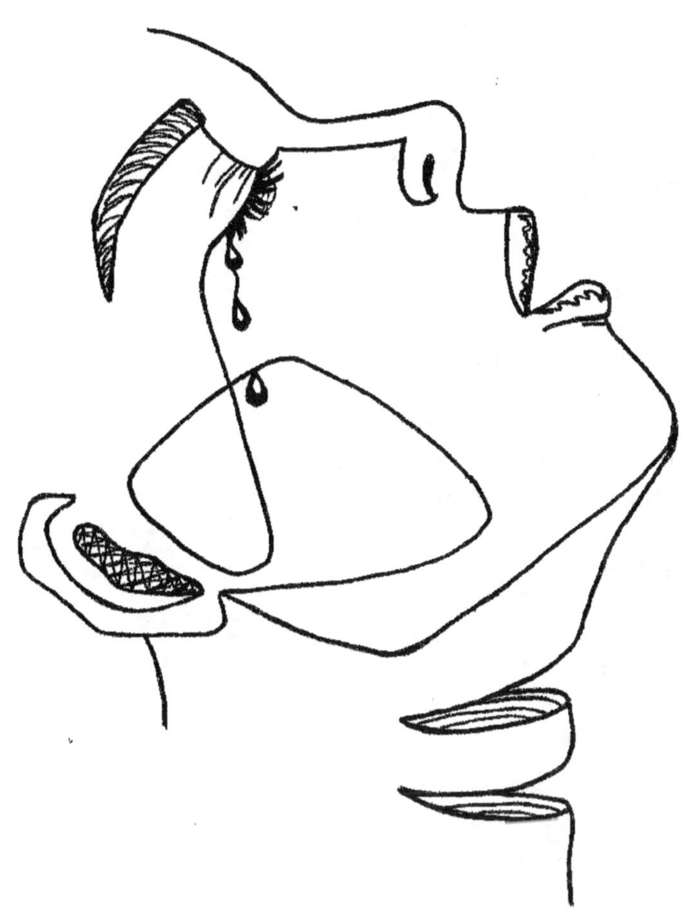

Isn't it?

I'm so thankful that I didn't end up
with what I thought I wanted.
Parched lips crave the rain
until they realise they're drowning.

Suspended underwater
sinking in slow motion.
Fractured light and burning lungs
so picturesque in the silence.
Self sacrifice and distorted lies,
isn't it romantic?

I'm so thankful I didn't end up
with what I thought I wanted.
A candle alone in the dark
works twice as hard to provide light
to the one who set it alight.

Burning out
Giving in.
Burnout.
Isn't it romantic?

Without

I have so many dreams
and to live without is empty
is cold
is not enough -

Stretched

Time tries to claim me.
The past, present and future,
shifting between their realities,
fighting for control.
The past holds me back
the future pulls me forwards
and I am s t r e t c h e d .

We are all stuck in the past -
it grasps us
until we process and overcome,
evolve
and move on.
Shedding old shadows -
how unique we are in this world.

The future is more sly.
Robbing us of our present
by presenting us with unwelcome gifts
of fears and what ifs.
Why worry about tomorrow
when today has enough worries
of its own?

You do not belong to the past,
and the future will come to you.
Be here.
Choose now.
Breathe.

Let me out

Take a walk inside your mind,
down darkened streets
under flickering lights.
Open up the hidden doors and dare to explore
the secret things you've tucked away,
out of reach of the light of day.
You've kept me safe,
you've taken the weight,
carried it all with a straight face,
but can you hear me calling now?
It's time to let me out.

Let me out
of me.

I am ready to feel again.

Read at your own risk.

I am more than a footnote
in his story,
not just another reference for his dating history.
How can I be reduced to so little
when he has taken up chapters of me?

I'm not to be left, stood on some shelf
gathering dust, all by myself.

I am a whole damn book to be loved and cherished,
so take me in your hands and turn my pages.
Highlight and underline your favourite parts,
memorise until you know me by heart.

In me are written riddles and rhyme,
won't you take the time to decipher me?
Will you dare to leave your mark,
write your name across my heart?
Engraved forever in this story -

What will I be to you?
A line? A paragraph? A chapter?
A fond memory, or a happy ever after?
I am more than a footnote,
I'm a vibrant character,
I won't be reduced to a couple of letters.
Take good heed and read me at your own risk
putting me down may be harder than you think.

How to compliment me:

Tell me I look like a writer. That I'm beautiful, not just pretty. Send me an Instagram post that made you think of me. Tell me you enjoyed the time we spent together. Let me know you can't wait to see me again. Learn my love languages; quality time, words of affirmation, touch. Tell me you don't think I'm too much; that you love my colours the way they are, that they shouldn't be dimmed, dulled or barred. Reach out to me first, am I on your mind? I'm not one to assume I occupy the thoughts of others once I'm gone – memories of me surely get left behind? I know I'm warm and expressive, I give the illusion of being open but the truth is – its rare I show the fullness of me. And so the greatest compliment would be if you took the time to look inside, to gain my trust, not too slow, not too rushed. Take interest and invest in me. Understand me. Make me feel seen and believed in. And maybe let me see you too? I'm interested in people. I'm interested in you.

Literary sketch

One day, if I can find the right words,
I'll paint your smile.
I'll sketch you in metaphors,
creating images and scenes
you've never seen before.
Take a look through my eyes,
take a look inside my mind;
I'll use my best vocabulary
of colours and similes
to capture you.
It won't do you justice
but I'll do my best
to immortalise us
and make art of us both.
The poet and the poem.

Camouflaged Heart

Take apart my soul
and lay my pieces down.
Loosen all my masks,
peeling back the layers exposed to
you
until you reach the centre.
Find my camouflaged heart
falling apart
under your touch.
Please be gentle.

I vowed.

I knew when I vowed to live a creative life
that there would be consequences.

Time. Money. Perseverance.
For these I was prepared, I expected even -
and yet it seems there was more.

I have learnt that to live a creative life
is to live wholeheartedly as yourself,
showing your vibrant colours to all you meet -
not dimming the lights for those who find you too bright.
You are not too much, I promise.
In every area of life let passion seep
into all you do.
Including the way you love -
It turns out I have a lot of love to give.

I often find it bursting at the seams
until it seems
       I am overflowing
              and I give away
parts of my heart with the best intentions
to people who don't value me the same.

And now I find myself on a precipice
wanting, needing, to throw myself
over the edge
but having stepped off this ledge before
I'm now more wary of what's at the bottom.

I must hold back, against all instinct,
all desire,
to protect myself.

Little Red

It hurts.
These ties and binds
are biting
and I don't know
what's worse.
Stepping back

       or stepping off.

When I say I'm falling for you, I mean:

I'm scared. I've felt like this before and I know how it ends. I mean: will you write us a different story? I mean: *are you different to the others?* I mean: *am I going to get hurt?* I mean: *I'm walking a tightrope with no safety net.* I mean: *I'm wrapping myself in bubble wrap. pop at your own risk – and for the love of God do it slowly.* I mean: *I'm sat on the side of the pool, dipping my toes in. now my legs. I can't remember how to swim.* I mean: *I'm not good at this.* I mean: *here is a shovel; will you excavate or bury me? I haven't dated in so long I feel like an artefact.* I mean: *I swallowed a butterfly. or ten.* I mean: *you don't need a stethoscope to hear how loud my heart is beating.* I mean: *I'm a rose. be careful of my thorns.* I mean: *I come with a warning label; HANDLE WITH CARE.* I mean: *your smile makes me feel safe. you make me laugh. I want to spend all my time with you. is that enough?* I mean: *I want to hold your hand.* I mean: *do you feel the same?*

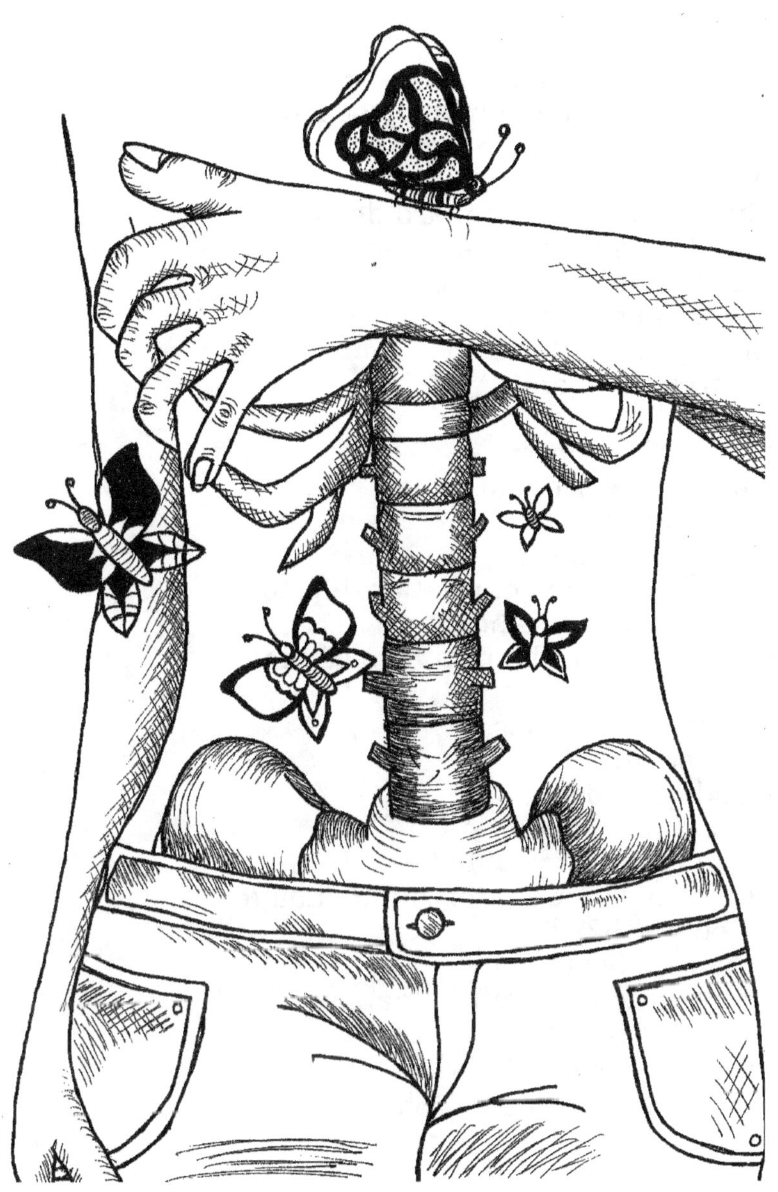

State lines

Respect my boundaries –
these fences, crackling with electricity.
They keep me in
as much as others out.
Is it about time I let my guard down?
I dug these trenches for a reason
and I'm still cleaning the blood and dirt
from under my fingers.
Unlearning old patterns,
healing from triggers.

Meet me at the border
between your world and mine –
to bridge this gap
will take trust and time.
The charred remains of relationships past
have at last stopped smoking.
The skies are grey, the rains are coming.

Respect my boundaries
but don't be afraid
to try and get close,
I'd like it if you stayed.
If you wanted to. If you'd like.
Do you like me? Am I interesting enough?
Is this too much?
I don't know how to act.
How to react to this shift in me.
This change from self defence
to exploring new possibilities.

Little Red

I'm scared. I'm lost. Am I enough?
What if I'm not?
What if I get hurt?
Again. Again. Again.
I hear you calling my name.

Stay back –

Stay.

Would you listen?

I've discovered a dangerous thing:
I want to share my poetry
with you.
A three pointed sign in fluorescent red light.
But am I warning myself or you?

I want to be vulnerable again.
Long-silenced truths on the edge of my tongue.
How have you convinced me to reveal parts of myself
I only share from behind anonymity -
without saying a single word?

I want to share my poetry with you
but I hold back.
First I need to be sure that you will listen.
Even if you don't understand at first.

So instead I show you music.
If I can't share my words
perhaps you'll hear me
perhaps you'll see me
in the songs I share with you.

After all the butterflies

With each page of you I turn
a butterfly earn it's wings
and flutters away -
and I am uncertain what remains.
Up till now, crushes have been
stomach twists and daydreams
but now it seems
'in like' is taking on a new form.
It's less ambiguous and more realistic.
I know what I'd like and I'm willing
to ask for it (I think).
It's enjoying your company
and learning about your history.
You tell me about your insecurities
as well as the ways you'd like
to improve yourself.

It's stepping off a ledge
but this time I'm wearing a parachute.
Directing my fall while enjoying
the view.
When I look at you, what I see
is no longer a kaleidoscope
but a mosaic.
My vision no longer distorted
I see the pieces, the cracks, the faults -
and I'm okay with them.
I'm not scared.
I'm not put off.
I see you as you are – and I want you anyway.
And perhaps after all the butterflies fly away -
this is what remains.

Less is not always more

I will not dim my mind,
dumb down what's inside,
so a man may feel more comfortable
in my presence.
I will not make myself less
just to impress another
with my silence,
again.
I will not dull my colours.
I will not hide
I will not disguise
her.
I.
She.
We.
Anxiety is a part of me,
though not permanently,
but I will not be ashamed
and I will not live any less brightly for it.
I am colourful,
I am creative,
I am messy -
this chaos contains some of the best parts of me,
and I trust the right people
(or person)
will see that.

Roaring tides

This poet hopes that her words will outlive her,
passed between the lips of generations.
Ever distorted from her original manuscript,
yet still retaining her essence.

She hopes that her words will inspire someone,
that their heart may swell and for a moment
believe in the impossible
and create something beautiful.

She does not fear death
but instead the way souls subtly fade from this world.
Erased as easily as waves wash away
footprints in the sand.
Their voices lost in the roar of the tide.

Don't forget me.

Spring Cleaning

Her colours are changing.
Don't ask her to stop.
She's cleaning the stains of muted grey
she's painted herself with for so long.
She had to be strong, get through, carry on,
stuck in survival mode -
on the edge of emotional overload.

She was too red, too blue, too much.
So she masked herself in grey,
put the pain away,
archived in the back of her mind.
On hold. Gathering dust.
This mask was a complicated disguise
projected both externally and inside
until even she became blind to her own
depths.
A misguided attempt at self defence.

Now as she cleans it seems that
the red and blue have bruised over,
she is covered in purple wounds
that will only heal when acknowledging the truth.
Now that she can breathe,
no longer bleeding,
she has the emotional capacity
to investigate these tragedies,
reclaim her identity
and bring it into the light.

<h1 style="text-align:center">Little Red</h1>

The colours of me are changing,
perhaps the beginning of healing.
Purple, blue, yellow.
Don't ask me to stop.

Chapter three

My mind is littered with half written sentences.
Unfinished. Lying dormant.
Half alive in this half light,
chapters of my life have been stranded on a cliffhanger,
without punctuation to bring me closure.

I acknowledge, I process, but only to the point the stress
subsides
and I'm no longer in survival mode.
These ghosts have made a home
in the back streets of my consciousness.
No map to guide, I can only look inside
and confront what I find when I turn these pages.

Chapter one:

I love them, my family, but the egg shells are crumbling
my feet are bleeding, but I keep on cleaning
the mess and supporting them
the best I can, but my back is sore and my heart is heavy,
I'm growing up too fast, I'm sorry.
I moved away. I'm sorry. But the hurt is still-

Next.

Chapter 2:

He loved me. He left me. He used me. He hurt me. He took
my-

Next.

Little Red

These visits are causing unrest.
Gentle cries inside my head,
these ghosts are groaning "God, help me".
Perhaps now is the time to reach out and get help.
Shed light on the monsters so they may finally rest.
I'm not good at asking for it,
but help seems to be the only way forward.
So I will try.

Chapter 3:

Trailblazer

I am light.
At least that's what my name means.
Bright light.
A trail blazer in the darkest night.

But who am I to lead the way,
to bring others into the dawn of day?

Who am I to give advice
when I can barely see out
of my own crises?

Who am I to say that I am wise,
when I have fallen for deception disguised
as love?
As hope?

And yet I must believe that I am a future flame,
but for now a spark.
I will endeavour to terrify the dark
and stretch out a hand to those around me.
Those who follow in my footsteps,
I set them free
from my past mistakes
in the hope they will overtake
and run farther than I ever could.

I will love
and lose
and love again

and maybe, *maybe* then
the light I store so deep inside
will start to seep through my eyes,
ignite a flame or brighter still
and continue to burn forever-

or at least until
your shadows are no more.

Be with me

Be with me, I ask,
like the reality
is that you'd ever leave my side.
I once tried to leave yours -
but you followed me into even
the darkest places.
I cannot hide from you.

Be with me, I ask.
Without you I fall apart.
When anxiety creeps in
and the wolves are all around,
surround me with your heart,
hide me within.
My safe place.

Be with me.

Today I felt the most me I have ever been.
I felt confident, I felt seen.
What a relief, to finally like this girl.
Today I looked inside and opened a door
and through the threshold I saw
the woman I'm becoming
and she is beautiful.
She wears a smile and she wears it well.
It's all because of you.

Be with me.
My best efforts are so cold, so feeble,
without you I am unable to do anything.
How freeing that your love is not dependent
on my strength, my attempts.

Little Red

In you all things are possible
and I can stand tall
because you love me
because you love me
because you love me.
And this is my story.

Be with me.

You took all my guilt and shame,
died and rose again,
so every day I may live in the wonder
that you would sacrifice everything
just to be close to me,
to get to know me,
and I you.

Be with me.
All my hope is in you.
All my hope,
in this man,
in your plan,
to save the world.

Be with me,
is your invitation.
You say,
trust, believe,
and you will see
that although life will not be easy,
you will never be alone.

Be with me.

Neverland

Hold on to stardust dreams
when reality starts picking at the seams
of the abstract scenes playing in your mind.

Don't let the sun rise melt the sleep
from your eyes,
linger in this limbo a little longer.

Hovering between stars and sea
let the lull of the waves carry you back to me.

This place between wake and sleep,
this place where you still remember dreaming,
is where I'll always love you,
is where I'll always be waiting.

Second star to the right
and straight on till morning.

Little Red

Index

Emergence

Acknowledgements

Firstly, I would like to thank you for reading Little Red. It means more to me than I can say that you were interested enough to spend time reading this book. Thank you for allowing me to share my experiences and heart with you.

I would also like to thank the people who inspired some of these poems, not that you necessarily know who you are, but for better or worse you led to me discovering more about myself and enabled me to develop as a writer. These poems represent some of the things I wish I had been able to say. To those of you I have lost touch with, wherever you are now, I sincerely hope that you are happy and well.

I am so grateful for all the support I have received leading up to releasing this book. I am thankful to my friends who have encouraged me and been people I first shared my writing with. I am also immensely grateful to the First Line Poets community; your creativity, love and guidance has enabled this book to become a reality.

About the author

Ellie Craner is a 23 year old writer and artist from Kent, England. In 2021 she completed a BSc in psychology which explored her interest in mental health, anxiety, and other topics. In her writing she uses stories as a way to create new characters and worlds, as well as processing her own experiences.

When Ellie isn't working, she can be found painting, drumming, dancing or reading.

Little Red is Ellie's debut collection of poetry.

Little Red